TODAY'S WORLD

ENERGY AND LIGHT

PETER LAFFERTY

SHOOTING STAR PRESS

CONTENTS

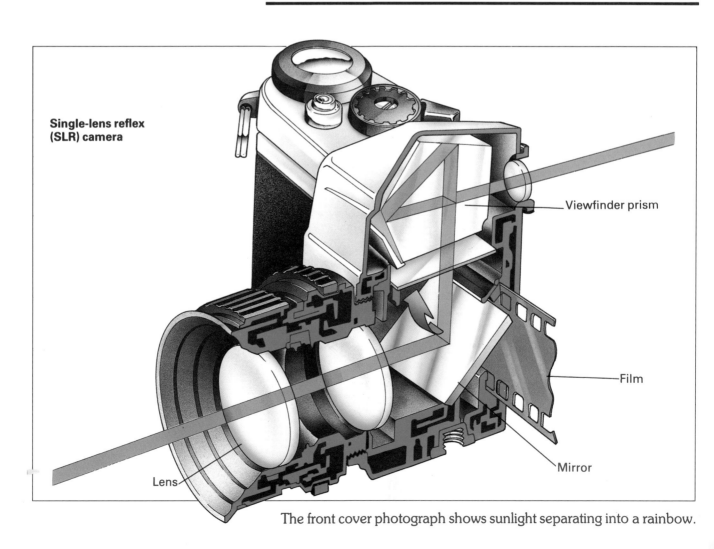

Single-lens reflex (SLR) camera

Viewfinder prism

Film

Lens

Mirror

The front cover photograph shows sunlight separating into a rainbow.

INTRODUCTION

Everything around us — the trees and rocks, the people and animals, the cars and houses, even the air and water — are made up of different kinds of material known as matter. This book looks at the ways in which matter can change from one form to another through the use of energy. Energy makes things happen – in scientific terms, it is the capacity to do work. Animals need energy to grow and move about, and they get their energy from the chemical substances in food; they make use of chemical energy. Machines also need energy to make them work; they use mechanical energy. And there are several other kinds of energy, including heat, light, sound, electrical energy and nuclear energy. Many forms of energy can be changed into each other. Electrical energy, for example, is converted into heat in an electric heater and into light in an electric lamp. The mechanical energy used in hitting a drum or a gong is converted into sound energy. Light is part of a whole family of radiant energy, which includes radio waves, ultraviolet light and X rays. All of them can be made by converting electrical energy. In all such conversions, no energy is ever lost, it is merely changed.

A laser is a concentrated beam of light.

Solids, liquids and gases

In a solid, the molecules or atoms are close together. They can make only small movements.

In a liquid, the atoms or molecules are farther apart. They can move around, but cannot break completely free from each other.

In a gas, the molecules or atoms are far apart and move very quickly, bouncing off the walls of their container.

Solid

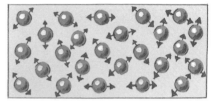

Liquid

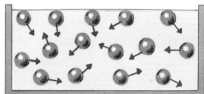

Gas

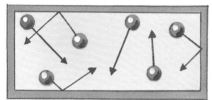

Gases
A gas has no definite shape or size, because its molecules are moving freely in all directions. When the gas is heated, the gas molecules move even faster, and the gas expands. The heated air inside the balloon is less dense than the air outside, making the balloon rise.

Changing states under pressure
A large amount of gas can be stored in a small pressurized container because under pressure gases turn to liquids. When the pressure on the liquid is released it again becomes a gas that can be burned.

Solids
A solid has a definite shape and size, because its molecules have fixed positions and cannot move about freely. The molecules in a solid are strongly attracted to each other.For this reason, metals and most other solids are strong materials.

MATTER

There are many different substances in the world – air, water, soil and grass, for example. These things are all different kinds of material, or matter.

The different kinds of matter have one thing in common, they are all made up of very small particles called atoms. In most common substances, the atoms are joined together in groups called molecules. In certain substances, known as chemical elements (such as oxygen, gold or calcium), the atoms are all the same. But in others, the molecules are made up of different atoms. For instance, a molecule of sugar is made up of carbon, hydrogen and oxygen atoms, whereas a molecule of water contains only hydrogen and oxygen atoms. The way in which the molecules are arranged determines whether the substance is a gas, a liquid or a solid. These are known as the three states of matter.

Surface tension

A small insect can rest on the surface of a still pond. Its legs make small dimples in the surface, which looks as if it were covered by a thin skin. This effect, called surface tension, happens because of the attraction between molecules of water at the surface.

Small droplets of water are often spherical and look as if they were held together by a thin skin. Water molecules at the surface of the drop are pulled towards the inside, so the surface area is as small as possible. The shrinking force is also caused by surface tension.

Breaking the rule
Most liquids take up less space, or contract, when they freeze. But water is an exception – it expands when it freezes. This is why expanding ice can burst water pipes in frosty weather, and why ice is less dense than water and floats on the tops of ponds, rivers and oceans.

Liquids
Unlike solids, liquids do not have a definite shape – they always take on the shape of the container that holds them. This is because their molecules are not tightly held together, which is also why they flow easily.

Surface tension   Insect floats on surface film

MASS AND WEIGHT

Units: Mass is measured in kilograms (abbreviation kg). Weight is measured in newtons (abbreviation N). One newton is about the weight of a large apple.

Weight is caused by the force of gravity acting on a mass. This force varies with distance from the center of the Earth.

The total amount of matter in an object is called its mass. A stone has more mass than an apple of the same size because the atoms and molecules in the stone are more tightly packed together. The individual atoms in the stone will weigh more than those in the apple too. The same volume of gas has hardly any mass at all, because it contains relatively few atoms. The weight of an object depends on its mass – the greater the mass, the heavier it is. For instance, a balloon filled with water is heavier than a balloon full of air, and a stone the size of a balloon is almost too heavy to pick up.

Force of gravity

If you pick up a stone and let it go, it falls to the ground. This happens because there is a force, called the force of gravity, pulling the stone towards the center of the Earth. Gravity is a force that exists between any two objects – it makes them attract each other but its effects are not noticeable unless one of the objects is very massive. The Earth and the Moon have very large masses. The gravitational attraction between them keeps the Moon in orbit around the Earth. It also affects the Earth's oceans and causes the tides.

The Earth's gravity keeps space satellites in orbit around the Earth, and stops them from flying off into space. Satellites are carried into space by a rocket because they must move very fast to be in orbit — if they go too slowly, they fall back to Earth. The gravitational attraction between the Sun and the planets, including the Earth, keeps the planets in orbit around the Sun.

An Ariane rocket lifts a satellite into space.

Earth's gravity holds satellites in orbit.

Gravity and weight

You can feel the pull of gravity every time you lift something. The force is called the weight of the object, which is the Earth's gravitational force on the object. Its magnitude depends on the distance between the object and the center of the Earth. For this reason, if you weighed yourself in an aircraft flying at a high altitude, you would find that you weigh slightly less than you do on the ground. If you went to the Moon, you would be affected by the Moon's gravity. The Moon is less massive than the Earth so its force of gravity is weaker than Earth's. As a result, you would weigh much less on the Moon – only about one-sixth of your "Earth" weight.

On a spaceship going to the Moon, thousands of miles from the Earth and outside its gravitational field, you would be completely weightless. But in all places — on Earth, the Moon and in space — your mass would remain the same.

Everything on Earth has weight due to gravity.

The Moon has gravity one-sixth of the Earth's.

Earth's gravity

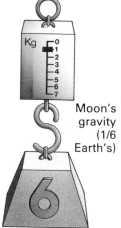
Moon's gravity (1/6 Earth's)

Center of gravity

All objects have a center of gravity, the point at which all their mass seems to act. A human being's center of gravity is in the middle of the body, roughly between the hips. When you are standing upright, gravity pulls on your center of gravity along a line that passes through your feet. But if you lean over far to one side so that the line is outside your feet, your center of gravity shifts and you will overbalance.

A double-decker bus is built with a very low center of gravity so that there is no danger of it toppling when it leans over on corners, even when most of the passengers are riding on the top deck. Buses are tested by being tilted over, to make sure they are safe under loaded conditions.

A bus undergoing a mechanical tilt check

FORCE AND MOMENTUM

Objects falling to the ground are accelerated by the force of gravity, gaining an extra 9.8 meters (32ft) per second of downward speed every second. This is called the acceleration due to gravity. The size of a force is measured in newtons (see page 34).

A force is a push or a pull which can make an object move, or change direction, or change the speed at which it is moving. Thus, when you push a supermarket cart, it moves. If you continue to push it with the same force, the cart speeds up – it accelerates. If, when the cart is moving, you stop pushing and let it go, it continues to move, but it soon slows down because of the frictional forces acting on it, and then it stops. If there were no frictional forces, the cart would continue to move at the same speed until some other force acted on it.

Simple machines

Machines are used to do work. They are designed to increase the effect of a force. There are various kinds of simple machines, including levers, pulleys, gears and screw threads. In each of them, a small force, called the effort, is used to overcome a larger force, called the load. There are three different kinds of levers shown here, each with the pivot, or fulcrum, in a different position. In each case, a small force can lift a large weight. A pulley uses rope wrapped around wheels in a certain way to lift heavy weights with only a small pull. Each stretch of rope carries the force that is exerted by the pull. For example, when four pulleys are used, the weight is shared among four stretches of rope and the force you need is only a quarter of what you would need to lift the weight by yourself. Gears are toothed wheels that are used to speed up or slow down a rotating wheel. In a bicycle, gears are used to transfer forces from the pedals to the wheels.

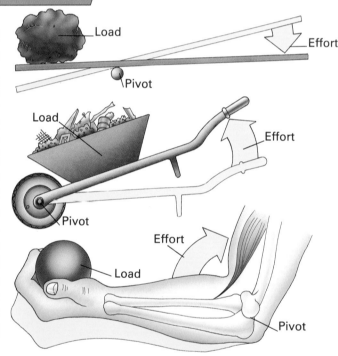

Giant cranes make use of pulleys.

A bicycle may have several gears.

Speed and acceleration

Speed is a measure of how fast something is moving – it is the distance moved by an object in a certain time. If a car takes an hour to travel 80 km (50 miles), dividing the distance by the time gives the average speed of the car over the whole journey, in this case 80 km/h (50 mph). At any moment during the trip, the car may be moving faster or slower than the average speed, and sometimes it may be stationary. Sometimes the car may be moving at a steady speed, and sometimes it may be speeding up or slowing down. When it is changing speed, the car is said to be accelerating; acceleration is the rate at which something changes speed. A car or any other moving object cannot change speed or accelerate without being pushed or pulled by a force. To make a car accelerate, the engine produces a greater force when the driver presses the accelerator (gas) pedal. On an aircraft carrier, a large catapult provides sufficient force to accelerate planes to their flying speed.

A catapult accelerates a plane to flying speed.

Momentum

A force is needed to stop a moving object, such as a car, because the car has momentum. Momentum depends on both speed and mass. If a car is moving at high speed, it has more momentum than when it is moving at a slow speed. For this reason, a greater force is needed to stop a fast-moving car. It also takes a greater force to stop a heavy truck than a small car – the truck has greater momentum because it has more mass.

When objects collide, their total momentum does not change. Sometimes at pool, when the moving cue ball hits a stationary ball, the cue ball stops. The second ball moves off at the same speed as the cue ball had. The momentum of the first ball has been transferred to the second ball (below, left). In a pile driver, the momentum of a massive falling weight is transferred to a smaller pile, which is gradually driven into the ground.

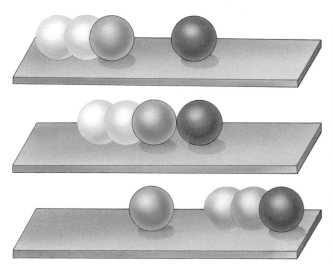

A pile driver makes use of momentum.

ENERGY

Any form of energy can be converted into a different form. For instance, a ball rolling down a hill loses potential energy, but gains kinetic energy.

Although energy cannot be destroyed, the amount of useful energy is always reduced when energy changes form. Waste heat, which cannot be converted to useful work, is produced. For example, in a radio, which changes electrical energy into sound, some of the energy is changed into heat in the wires and is lost.

There are many different forms of energy, which are needed to do any kind of work. We need energy to carry out any task, and we get it from our food where it is stored as chemical energy. Green plants get their energy from the Sun as heat and light, and they store it in chemical form. If the plants decay and change into coal or oil, the chemical energy is held in the coal or oil. But it can be released as heat and light energy when the fuel is burned. The heat produced may be used to generate electricity, another form of energy and probably the most useful in today's world. A moving object also has energy, and so does a wound-up clock spring. A kind of energy that has always been around but only recently has been exploited is nuclear energy. This can be produced in nuclear reactors by the splitting of atoms of elements such as uranium.

Potential and kinetic energy

If you lift a heavy book up high, you use energy to do it. But the energy does not vanish. It remains in the book as stored energy – called potential energy – and can be released if you let the book fall. A bent bow also has potential energy. The archer does work to pull back the bow-string, and the energy used is stored in the bent bow. When the archer lets go of the string, the energy is released and shoots the arrow through the air.

As the arrow flies through the air it has another kind of energy. This is known as kinetic energy, or energy due to motion. As the arrow hits the target, the target moves slightly as the arrow gives up its kinetic energy. A hammer or pneumatic drill also uses kinetic energy, which may be enough to pound in a nail or smash concrete. The amount of energy depends on the mass and speed of the hammer or drill.

A drawn bow stores potential energy.

A pneumatic drill uses kinetic energy.

This inventor is trying to make a perpetual motion machine, which is one that will go on forever without needing a source of power. He first boils water using an electric stove connected to a battery. The steam produced drives a turbine connected to an electric generator. The electricity from the generator works the bell and lights the lamp before going to the battery to recharge it. The inventor thinks there should be enough electrical energy arriving at the battery to keep it completely charged. The invention will not work, however. The inventor has forgotten that energy is lost because waste heat is produced at several places. Heat is produced in the turbine and generator because of friction between their moving parts. Heat is also produced in the wiring inside the electric bell, and heat and light are produced by the lamp. Because of these losses, the battery is not completely recharged and the machine will eventually come to a halt when the battery is dead.

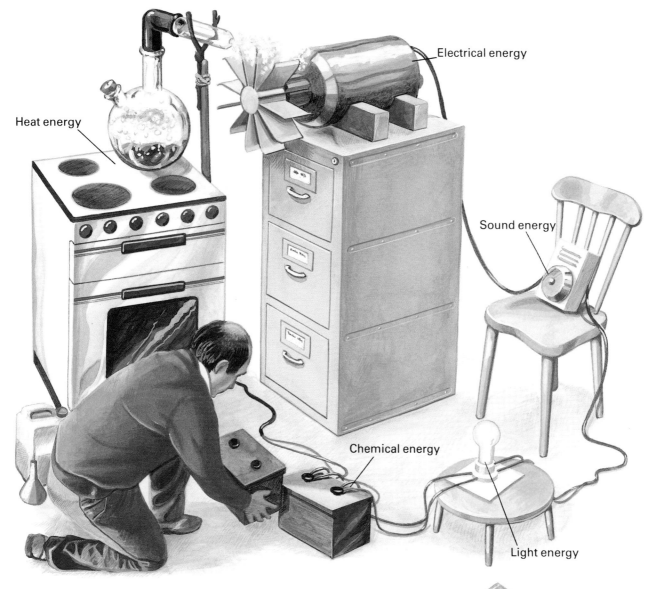

Heat energy

Electrical energy

Sound energy

Chemical energy

Light energy

A pendulum is a continuous energy converter. At each end of its swing it is stationary and has potential energy. As it swings it loses potential energy and gains kinetic energy, which is greatest at the bottom of the swing when it is moving fastest. If it were not for air resistance and friction in the suspension, it would go on swinging forever in perpetual motion. But because of energy losses, it gradually slows down.

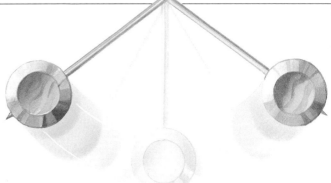

VIBRATING PARTICLES

There are two main temperature scales: Celsius and Fahrenheit. On the Celsius scale, water freezes at 0° C and boils at 100° C. On the Fahrenheit scale, it freezes at 32° F and boils at 212° F. The lowest possible temperature is -273.16° C (-459.69° F), which is called absolute zero.

When something is heated, the atoms or molecules in it begin to move faster. The hotter an object is, the quicker its molecules are moving. The colder it is, the slower they are moving. Heat is therefore a form of energy – it is the kinetic energy of moving molecules.

Temperature is a measure of hotness, so heat and temperature are not the same thing. For example, a burning match has a high temperature but gives out little heat. A household radiator, on the other hand, gives out a lot of heat although its temperature is not very high.

How heat travels

Heat can travel in three ways – by conduction, convection or radiation. Conduction is the way heat travels in a solid, such as a metal bar. If one end of the bar is heated, the molecules at the heated end start to vibrate more vigorously. The vibrations of the heated molecules are passed to neighboring ones, and the heat travels along the bar. Convection is the way heat travels in liquids and gases. A current of heated gas or liquid, called a convection current, starts to flow. The heat haze seen on a hot day is caused by currents of hot air rising from heated roads. Heat travels through space and air by waves of energy, called radiation. This is how heat reaches the Earth from the Sun, and keeps the Earth warm enough for life.

The Sun's radiant heat causes a suntan.

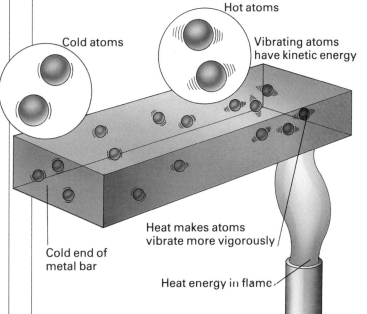

Cold atoms

Hot atoms

Vibrating atoms have kinetic energy

Heat makes atoms vibrate more vigorously

Cold end of metal bar

Heat energy in flame

Convection currents cause a heat haze.

Expansion

When something is heated and its molecules start vibrating faster, they take up more room. This is why most things expand, or get bigger, when they are heated. Gases expand a great deal when heated, which is why a small amount of heated air easily fills a hot-air balloon. Liquids also expand in this way. In a thermometer, a thin column of liquid (usually mercury or alcohol) expands as it is heated by its surroundings. The liquid moves up the hollow tube and indicates the temperature. Solids expand less than gases or liquids. Nevertheless bridge builders must leave small gaps in bridges so that they can expand without buckling in hot weather. Expansion joints are also left between the ends of the rails in railroad tracks. Telephone wires, slung between poles, sag on hot days because the wires expand and get longer in the heat.

A gap is left between rails to allow for expansion.

Thermometer (Celsius and Fahrenheit)

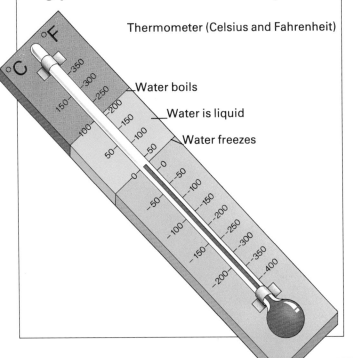

Water boils

Water is liquid

Water freezes

Vacuum flask

A vacuum flask or thermos bottle is for keeping hot liquids hot or cold liquids cold. It is designed so that heat cannot easily get in or out. It is made of glass and has thin, double walls. All the air is pumped out of the space between the walls, creating a vacuum. This is done so that heat cannot escape or enter by convection or conduction – there is no material between the walls to carry heat in or out. To prevent heat escaping as radiation, the sides of the flask have a silver coating, like a mirror. This reflects any radiated heat back into the flask, and prevents any radiation from entering it. The flask is held firmly in an outer container by insulated supports. The stopper in the flask is made of cork or plastic, both of which are poor conductors of heat. As a result, no heat can enter or be lost through the mouth of the flask. The vacuum flask was invented by the British scientist James Dewar, and is sometimes called a Dewar flask.

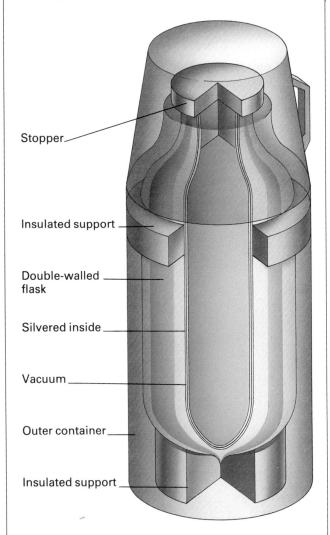

Stopper

Insulated support

Double-walled flask

Silvered inside

Vacuum

Outer container

Insulated support

Sound travels through air at a speed of 331.4 meters per second (750 mph). It travels faster through denser materials such as water or metals – 15 times as fast through steel, for example. The fastest military jet aircraft can fly at more than three times the speed of sound.

All sounds are made by something vibrating rapidly back and forth. For example, when you talk, your vocal cords vibrate. You can feel the vibrations if you place your finger lightly on the front of your neck while you speak. The vibrations cause pressure changes in the air, and these quickly spread out as sound waves, moving energy from one place to another. When the sound waves enter somebody's ear, they cause the eardrum to vibrate and the sound is heard because the energy has been transferred from your vocal cords to the other person's ear.

How sound travels

As a vibrating object moves forward, it pushes the air in front of it, creating a small region of high air pressure. When the object moves backward, it creates a region of low pressure. These high and low pressure regions travel out from the vibrating object as sound waves, like ripples on a pond. Sound can travel through other materials in much the same way, but it cannot travel through a vacuum. This is why astronauts wearing space suits have to use a radio to speak to each other. If the radio fails, they have to press their helmets together so that the sound travels through the materials of the helmets. Sound waves bounce off hard surfaces, causing echoes. In concert halls, echoes can distort the sound of the music. Often baffles are hung to absorb sound and prevent echoes.

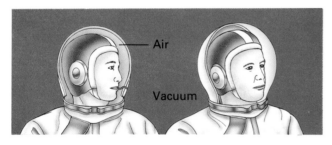

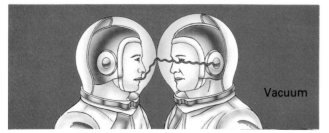

Ceiling baffles improve a concert hall's acoustics.

Sound levels

The loudness of a sound is determined by measuring the energy in the sound waves. The energy in a sound is measured in decibels. The softest sound that can be heard is about 0 decibels.

A whisper might be about 20 decibels. A loud noise, like a vacuum cleaner or record player, is about 70 decibels, and a very loud noise, like a motorcycle, might be about 100 decibels.

Sounds above 140 decibels are so loud that they can cause pain or even deafness. For this reason, people who work with noisy machinery are advised to wear ear protectors.

| Too quiet | | | | | | | | | | | | | Danger level | | |

-10 0 10 20 30 40 50 60 70 80 90 100 110 120 130 140 150 160 170 180 190 200

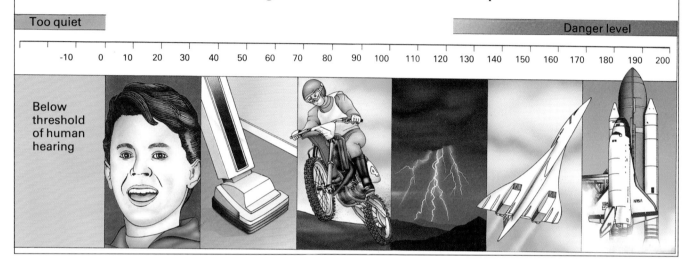

Below threshold of human hearing

Sound barrier

A supersonic aircraft, such as the Concorde, can fly faster than sound. When it does so, it has broken the sound barrier. As the aircraft flies at less than the speed of sound, the sound waves it causes have time to move aside the let the aircraft pass. As it approaches the speed of sound, it begins to "catch up" with the sound waves. But when it exceeds the speed of sound, the aircraft overtakes the sound it produces and the sound waves pile up on each other and create much more intense sound. This causes a loud bang, called a sonic boom, which can be heard on the ground. The shock waves of a sonic boom can break the windows of houses.

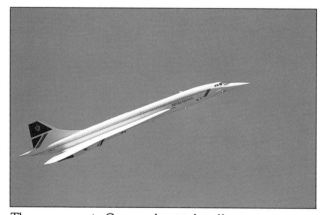

The supersonic Concorde at takeoff

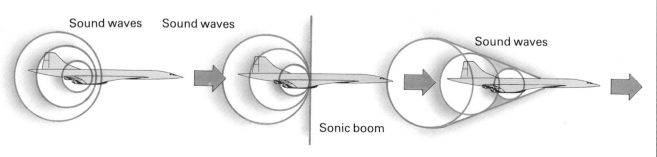

Sound waves   Sound waves   Sound waves

Sonic boom

Subsonic flight
(below speed of sound)   Flight at speed of sound   Supersonic flight
(above speed of sound)

ENERGETIC ELECTRONS

Atoms are small but the atomic nucleus is even smaller. If a nucleus were the size of a small coin, the whole atom would be the size of a skyscraper.

A nucleus is made up of protons and neutrons. Each is about 2,000 times heavier than an electron.

More than 2,000 years ago, a Greek scientist discovered that a type of fossil called amber could, after being rubbed with a silk cloth, attract small pieces of straw. He had discovered electricity. The attraction is caused by tiny, invisible particles of electricity called electrons, which occur inside the atoms and molecules that make up all substances. Normally an atom has an equal number of protons (with a positive charge) and electrons (with a negative charge). But when an object has more or less electrons than its normal number it has an electric charge, and can attract other objects.

Free electrons

Every atom has a central part called a nucleus, which is made up of particles called protons and neutrons. Around the nucleus, there are a number of electrons, normally the same as the number of protons in the nucleus. But it is possible for an atom to lose electrons or gain extra ones. When you comb your hair with a plastic comb, some electrons are rubbed off your hair and onto the comb. If you hold the comb close to your finger in the dark, you may see a small spark. This is also the extra electrons jumping from the comb to the finger. This is what happens, on a much larger scale, when lightning strikes. Extra electrons build up on the bottom of a cloud and after a while jump to Earth as a huge spark. One flash of lightning has enough power to start fires, split open a tree and kill people.

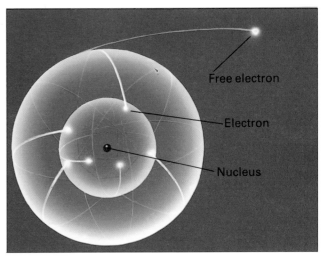

Diagram of an atom

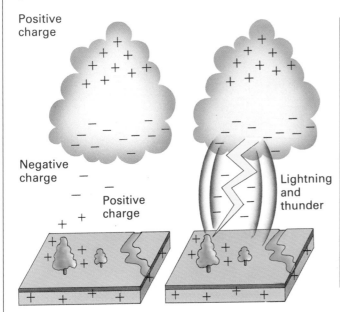

Lightning is a huge electric spark.

Van de Graaff generator

A Van de Graaff generator produces large electric charges for use in scientific experiments. It consists of a movable belt that is driven around a pair of rollers. At the lower end of the belt is a metal comb connected to the positive terminal of a powerful high-voltage supply. Small electric sparks shoot from the teeth of the comb and put positive charges onto the belt, which carries them to the top of the generator. There another metal comb lifts the charges off the belt and stores them on a polished metal sphere. After a while, a large charge builds up on the sphere. Van de Graaff generators are used to produce high-voltage electricity for testing insulators, or beams of charged atoms, called ions, which are used to smash atoms and investigate their makeup.

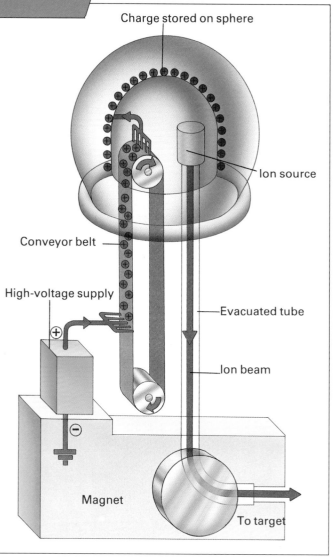
Charge stored on sphere
Ion source
Conveyor belt
High-voltage supply
Evacuated tube
Ion beam
Magnet
To target

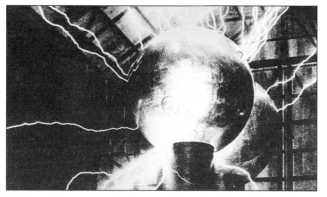
High-voltage sparks from a Van de Graaff generator

Attraction of opposite charges

The protons in the atomic nucleus are also electrically charged particles. But unlike negatively charged electrons they carry a positive charge. The neutron, the other kind of particle found in the nucleus, has no electric charge at all. A positive charge is attracted to a negative charge, but two positive charges – or two negative ones – do not attract each other. When an inflated balloon is rubbed on a woolen sweater, electrons transfer to the balloon and it becomes negatively charged. At the same time, the sweater becomes positively charged, because it now has more protons than electrons. The opposite charges attract each other, and the balloon sticks to the sweater. This type of electric charge is called static electricity.

An electrically charged balloon attracts paper.

DC current

An electric current is a flow of electrons along a wire. In 1831 the British scientist Michael Faraday noticed that if a wire is moved near a magnet, an electric current starts. This is the principle of the electric generator, or dynamo. A simple generator is built just like an electric motor (see opposite page). If the coil is turned between the poles of a magnet, a current flows in the coil and the split ring, or commutator, ensures that the current continues to flow in the same direction. This sort of electric current is called direct current, or DC.

A car generates its own electric supply.

A simple generator

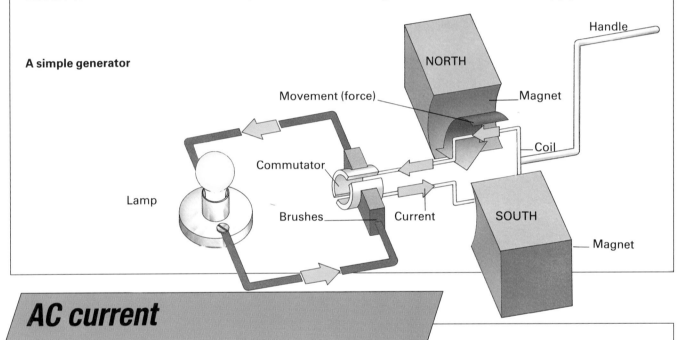

Lamp

Commutator

Brushes

Movement (force)

NORTH

Handle

Magnet

Coil

Current

SOUTH

Magnet

AC current

If the generator's commutator is replaced by complete rings connected to each end of the coil, a different type of current is produced. This current flows first in one direction and then in the opposite one, changing direction as often as the coil turns — about 50 or 60 times a second. It is called alternating current, or AC, and is the type of electricity used in homes.

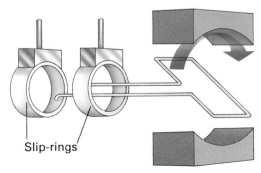
Slip-rings

Cables carry AC current from power stations.

Electric motors

When a wire carrying a current is brought near a magnet, it experiences a force and it moves. This is the principle of the electric motor. A motor consists of a coil of wire between the poles of a strong magnet. The coil is connected to a battery by means of a split ring, called a commutator, and brushes that press against it. As the coil turns, the commutator causes the current in the coil to reverse direction every half-turn of the coil. This keeps it turning in the same direction.

Electric motors are widely used in industry and around the home. They can be made very small to work a clock or a toy car, or large and powerful such as the huge motors that work the lifts that carry men and minerals up deep mine shafts. Unlike other kinds of motors they do not burn fuel and are pollution-free. For example, unlike diesels, electric railroad locomotives are clean and quiet.

Submarines also make use of electric motors to run silently underwater. Large batteries provide the electric power and are recharged by a generator when the submarine comes to the surface.

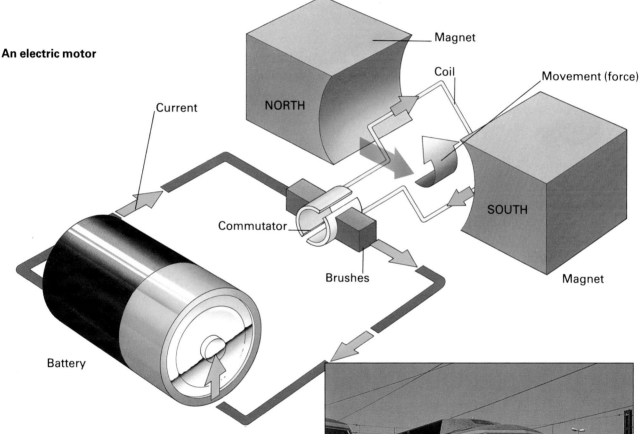

An electric motor

Magnet

Coil

Movement (force)

Current

NORTH

SOUTH

Commutator

Brushes

Magnet

Battery

Electric trains
Electric motors are used extensively to power streetcars and trains. With diesel electrics, the current is generated by a diesel engine and flows to the motor. The large modern express railroads, like the French T.G.V. (Train de Grande Vitesse — very fast train), collect the current from overhead cables through poles or pantographs. In other cases, where overhead wires are impractical or unsafe, a third rail carries the current and this is picked up by the engine.

The French electrical T.G.V.

The region around a magnet where its magnetism is effective is called a magnetic field. The Earth's magnetic field causes compass needles to point north. It also has an effect on some animals, such as migrating birds, which may use the Earth's magnetic field for navigation on long flights.

About 2,500 years ago, people discovered a black stone that could attract small pieces of iron. The stone, a type of iron ore called lodestone, was a naturally magnetic variety of the mineral magnetite. It also had another strange property. If a thin piece of lodestone was hung from a string, it would swing around and point toward north. Sailors began to use pieces of lodestone to navigate on long voyages. These were the first compasses. A compass needle does not, in fact, point to the North Pole, but instead it points to the magnetic north, a point in Northern Canada.

Magnets

All magnets have two regions, called poles, where the magnetism is strongest. One of them is called the north pole because, if the magnet can move, the north pole always turns towards north. The other, or opposite, pole is the south pole. If the same poles of two magnets are placed close together, they push apart, or repel each other. But the north pole of one magnet attracts the south pole of another one. The region around a magnet where the magnetic field can be felt is often drawn as "lines of force" which show the direction of the field around the magnet. A compass placed near a magnet points along the lines of force. The Earth acts like a huge magnet with its lines of force running in a north-south direction.

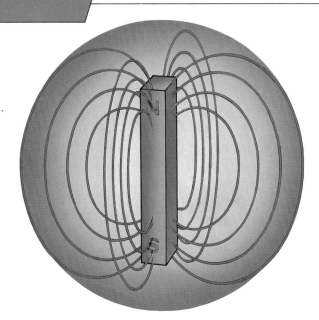

Lines of force

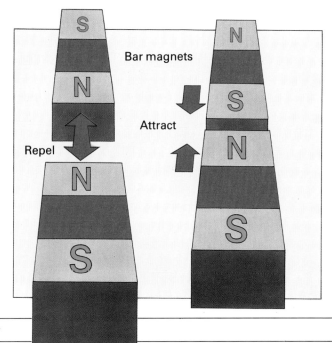

Bar magnets

Repel

Attract

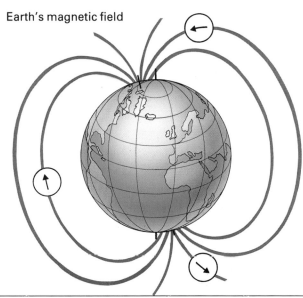

Earth's magnetic field

Electromagnets

Electricity and magnetism are very closely related. In 1819 a Danish scientist called Hans Christian Oersted discovered that a compass needle near a wire moves when an electric current passes along the wire. A much stronger magnetic effect is produced if the wire is wound into a cylindrical coil. Putting an iron rod inside the coil increases this electromagnetic effect even further – an insulated wire wrapped around an iron nail and connected to a battery makes a strong electromagnet. Electromagnets are convenient to use because their magnetism can be turned on and off by switching the electric current on and off.

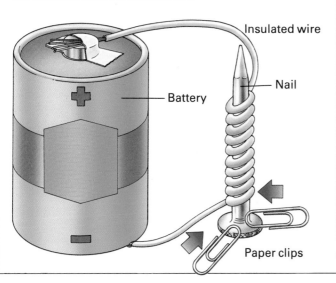

Insulated wire

Nail

Battery

Paper clips

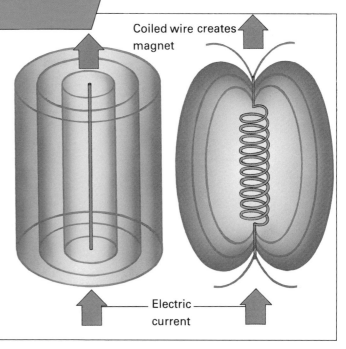

An electromagnetic crane lifting scrap steel

Big magnets

The largest and most powerful magnets in the world are superconducting magnets. They are electromagnets that are cooled to a very low temperature, near -270°C (-454°F). At this temperature, the wire in the coil of the magnet loses its resistance to the flow of electricity – it becomes superconducting. It is therefore possible to pass huge electric currents through the superconducting coil, producing a very strong magnet.

Superconducting magnets are used to control beams of particles in atom-smashing machines called particle accelerators. In an accelerator, the powerful magnetic fields guide the protons, electrons or other charged particles as they are accelerated and finally smash into their target atoms and split them.

Coiled wire creates magnet

Electric current

LIGHT ENERGY

Light travels at the fastest speed ever measured: 300,000 kilometers per second (about 186,000 miles per second). At this speed, light would take only one-tenth of a second to travel from New York to London. It takes 8 minutes to reach the Earth from the Sun, and 4.3 years to reach Earth from the next nearest star. Light travels as waves of extremely short wavelength.

Light is needed before you can see anything. If you shine a flashlight in a darkened room, you can see the objects that the flashlight's beam illuminates. The light falls on objects, bounces off them and some of the reflected light enters your eyes, enabling you to see the objects. You cannot see the beam of light produced by the flashlight, unless there are dust particles floating in the air. Then the dust reflects some of the light out of the beam and into your eyes.

White light, such as that from the Sun, consists of a mixture of colors — the colors of the rainbow. Light travels in straight lines – it will not go around corners. But it can be reflected (by a mirror) or bent (by a lens). Optical instruments such as microscopes, telescopes, cameras and projectors use mirrors and lenses to control light rays and form images that we can see.

What is light?

Light is electromagnetic energy. It can travel through air and other transparent substances, and through empty space. It can also be changed into other forms of energy – for example, an electric eye, or photocell, changes light into electricity. Light consists of a combination of electric and magnetic fields called electromagnetic waves. Radio waves, microwaves, infrared rays, ultraviolet light, X rays, and gamma rays are all other kinds of electromagnetic waves, but we cannot see them. They differ from visible light because they have different wavelengths. Radio, microwaves and infrared have longer wavelengths than light, whereas the wavelengths of ultraviolet, X rays and gamma rays are shorter. Some animals can "see" wavelengths that we cannot. For instance, certain snakes detect their prey using infrared rays.

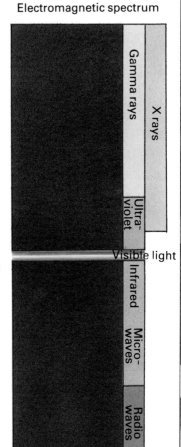

Electromagnetic spectrum

Gamma rays
X rays
Ultra-violet
Visible light
Infrared
Micro-waves
Radio waves

Wavelength increases

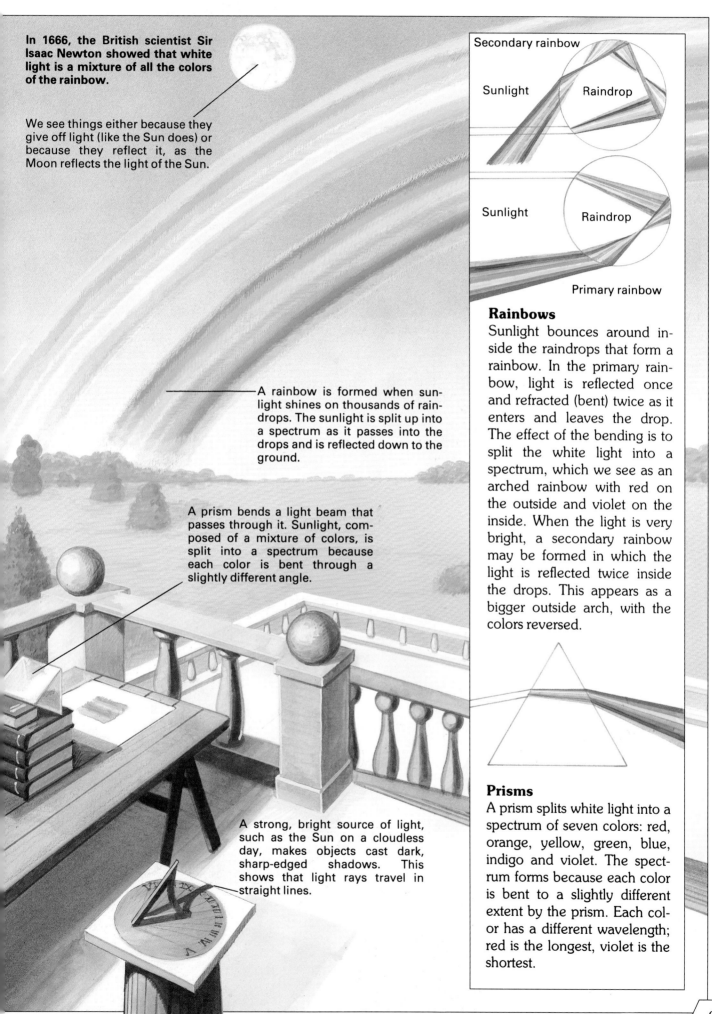

In 1666, the British scientist Sir Isaac Newton showed that white light is a mixture of all the colors of the rainbow.

We see things either because they give off light (like the Sun does) or because they reflect it, as the Moon reflects the light of the Sun.

A rainbow is formed when sunlight shines on thousands of raindrops. The sunlight is split up into a spectrum as it passes into the drops and is reflected down to the ground.

A prism bends a light beam that passes through it. Sunlight, composed of a mixture of colors, is split into a spectrum because each color is bent through a slightly different angle.

A strong, bright source of light, such as the Sun on a cloudless day, makes objects cast dark, sharp-edged shadows. This shows that light rays travel in straight lines.

Secondary rainbow

Sunlight

Raindrop

Sunlight

Raindrop

Primary rainbow

Rainbows

Sunlight bounces around inside the raindrops that form a rainbow. In the primary rainbow, light is reflected once and refracted (bent) twice as it enters and leaves the drop. The effect of the bending is to split the white light into a spectrum, which we see as an arched rainbow with red on the outside and violet on the inside. When the light is very bright, a secondary rainbow may be formed in which the light is reflected twice inside the drops. This appears as a bigger outside arch, with the colors reversed.

Prisms

A prism splits white light into a spectrum of seven colors: red, orange, yellow, green, blue, indigo and violet. The spectrum forms because each color is bent to a slightly different extent by the prism. Each color has a different wavelength; red is the longest, violet is the shortest.

Mixing colors

Paint of any color can be made by mixing the correct proportions of the three primary colors: red, blue and yellow. A mixture of roughly the same amounts of all three makes black, which can be considered as no color at all. But why does a red object look red or a green one green? Because the material from which it is made – or the paint it is painted with – absorbs all the colors from white light except red or green, which is reflected back to our eyes. A black object absorbs all colors and reflects none back. The primary colors do not have to be mixed; they can be separate small dots which are blended by our eyes and brain. That is the technique in the painting above. If you use a magnifying glass to look at this book, you will see tiny red, blue and yellow dots in each picture.

This painting is made up of tiny dots of pure color.

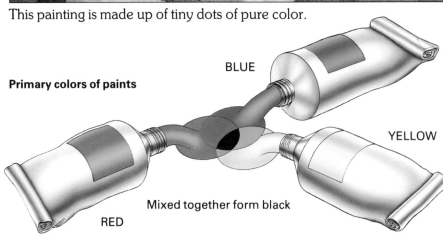

Primary colors of paints

BLUE

YELLOW

RED

Mixed together form black

Sources of light

Most light is produced by hot glowing objects such as the Sun or the filament of an electric lamp. But light can be produced in other ways. Some insects, such as fireflies and glowworms, give off light at night. The female firefly glows so that the male can find her. The glow is produced by chemicals inside her body. Many deep-sea fish also produce light in this way, which is called bioluminescence – luminescence is the term for the production of light without heat. The hands and numbers on some clocks and watches are coated with luminescent paint that glows in the dark.

Other chemicals that glow without heat are called phosphors, and they can produce light of various colors. Those painted on the inside of a fluorescent light tube produce white light similar to daylight. They glow when hit by charged particles (ions) produced inside the tube, and the glow forms the light.

Glowworms produce light from chemical reactions.

Mixing colored lights is not like mixing paints. Light also has its primary colors – red, green and blue – but they mix by adding together (not by absorbing color as paints do). The correct proportions of the three primary colors produce white light; any other color can be made by different mixtures. On a television screen, the colors are produced by dots or lines of colored phosphors, which glow when hit by a beam of electrons inside the television tube. Some glow red, some glow blue and some glow green. By directing electrons at the correct combination of phosphors, any color can be produced on the screen because your eye will blend the colors together. The colored lights in a theater are produced by putting a colored filter in front of a white light source. The colors mix as shown.

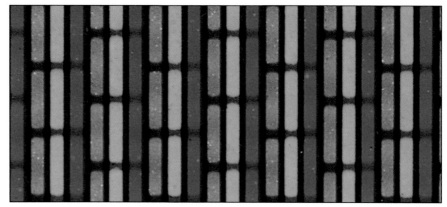

Close-up of a color television picture, showing phosphors

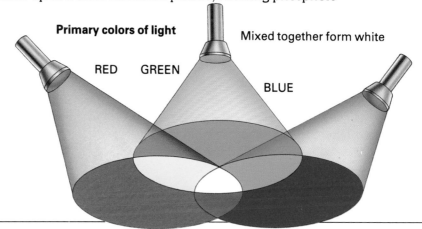

Primary colors of light

Mixed together form white

RED   GREEN

BLUE

Diffraction of light

The brilliant colors of a peacock's feathers are not caused by colored pigments. They arise because of very fine lines on the surface of the feathers which break up light falling onto them into a series of very thin beams or rays. The colors occur as the beams of the different colors interact. This causes some colors to be canceled and others to be made stronger. This is called diffraction. The different spectral colors that make up white light are spread by different amounts, and as they spread they mix to produce the brilliant colored patterns.

A similar rainbow of colors can be seen when a compact disc or videodisc is held at an angle to white light. This is also due to diffraction, and scientists make use of the effect in spectroscopes to split light into a spectrum. This enables them to identify chemical elements in a substance because each element has its own unique spectrum "fingerprint" that distinguishes it from others.

Light diffraction produces color in peacock feathers.

BOUNCING AND BENDING

Mirrors and lenses can reflect and refract light rays to form images. An image that can be focused onto a screen, like that produced by a slide projector, is called a real image. Other images, such as those produced by a microscope or a pair of binoculars, are called virtual images.

When light bounces off something it is reflected. Light is reflected best from shiny surfaces such as mirrors. When you look into an ordinary mirror, you see an image that is upright and the same size as the reflected object. But mirrors can be curved, like a car's driving mirror (which can produce a reduced image) or a shaving mirror (which produces a magnified image). Curved mirrors are also used in astronomical telescopes and other optical instruments. Many of these have lenses to enlarge the image produced by a mirror.

Reflection and refraction

When light is reflected from a flat surface, the angle at which it bounces off is the same as the angle at which it hits the surface. This is called the law of reflection of light. If you stand by a still pond, with someone on the opposite side, you can see, in the water, an upside-down image of the person on the other side. Because light normally travels in straight lines, the reflection appears to come from below the surface of the water.

When light passes from one transparent medium to another, it is bent, or refracted. For example, light is refracted when it passes from water to air. This is why a fish in a stream appears to be farther from the bank than it really is. In deserts, light is also refracted as it passes from cool air to hotter air near the ground. This forms a mirage in which images of water (which is only a refracted image of the sky) and trees appear to be much closer than they are.

The lake's surface acts as a huge mirror.

The upside-down trees and water are a mirage.

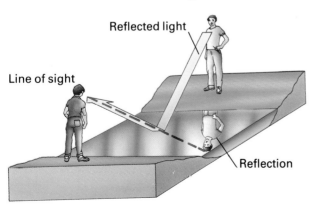

Reflected light

Line of sight

Reflection

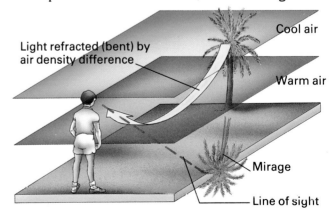

Cool air

Light refracted (bent) by air density difference

Warm air

Mirage

Line of sight

Convex and concave mirrors

Mirrors are smooth sheets of glass that have been painted on the back with a shiny metal — usually silver. The silver reflects light instead of letting it pass through the glass. The image reflected by any mirror is reversed as though the right side were the left and vice versa. But curved mirrors can also change the size of the image.

Convex mirrors are curved outward, like the back of a spoon. This shape allows them to collect light from objects that are far apart and reflect it to form a small upright image in the mirror. A good example of this is a car's rear-view mirror, which gives the driver a broad "picture" of the road behind. Concave mirrors are curved inward, like the front of a spoon. They produce an enlarged image of an object at close range. Mirrors used by people when shaving or putting on makeup are often concave mirrors.

In the diagrams, the solid red and blue lines represent light rays being reflected off an object into the mirror and back to your eye. The dotted lines show the way your eye would see the image — the light is reflected back at a different angle because the mirror is curved, and your eye would "see" the light as having come from a point at the end of a straight line (the focus). On a convex mirror the focus is behind the mirror; on a concave mirror it is in front of it. The image reflected is therefore smaller in a convex mirror. At close range in a concave mirror, the image is larger than the object, but when the object is further from the mirror the image is smaller and upside down.

A car's driving mirror is a convex mirror.

The bowl of a spoon acts as a concave mirror.

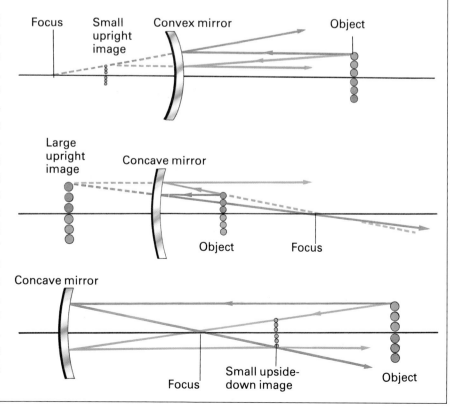

Glasses

Somebody who is nearsighted cannot see distant objects clearly. This is usually because the eyeball is too long. As a result, light entering the eyeball is not focused on the retina at the back of the eye, as it should be for clear vision, but is focused in front of it. To correct this problem, people can wear glasses or contact lenses with a concave lens, which cause a light beam to widen before entering the eye. Farsightedness occurs when light is focused behind the retina. It is corrected by a convex lens, which makes the light beam narrower before it enters the eye.

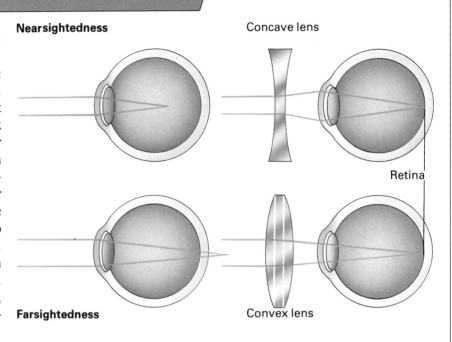

Nearsightedness

Concave lens

Retina

Farsightedness

Convex lens

Telescopes

Astronomical reflector telescope

A telescope was first used to study the heavens by Galileo in 1609. His simple telescope consisted of two lenses fitted at opposite ends of a hollow tube. A large convex (converging) lens at the front, called the objective lens, gathered in light and formed an upright image that was magnified by the eyepiece. The eyepiece consisted of a concave (diverging) lens. Opera glasses and binoculars still use a similar combination of lenses. Another type of telescope has two convex lenses. Astronomical telescopes that use lenses are called refractors. Other types, called reflectors, use mirrors to form images and most large telescopes are of this kind. The world's largest is in the Soviet Union; it has a mirror 6 m (nearly 20 ft) across. The largest refracting telescope has an objective lens 100 cm (39 in) across.

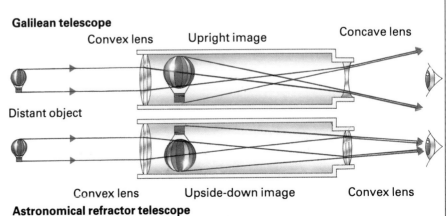

Galilean telescope

Convex lens   Upright image   Concave lens

Distant object

Convex lens   Upside-down image   Convex lens

Astronomical refractor telescope

The microscope

A microscope is used to look at objects, such as metal crystals and bacteria, that are so small they cannot be seen with the unaided eye. A very thin slice of the object being examined (which is known as a specimen) is placed on a glass slide. Light is reflected from a mirror below the specimen and passes through it to a very strong convex lens, the objective. This lens acts like a magnifying glass to form an enlarged image of the specimen. A second convex lens in the eyepiece magnifies the image even more. Modern microscopes use combinations of lenses in both the objective and the eyepiece to improve the clarity of the image. But there is a limit to the magnification possible with a microscope that uses light. Even greater magnifications are possible with an electron microscope, which uses a beam of electrons instead of light. Electromagnets, not lenses, focus the beam of electrons to form an image. Some electron microscopes are powerful enough to show individual atoms.

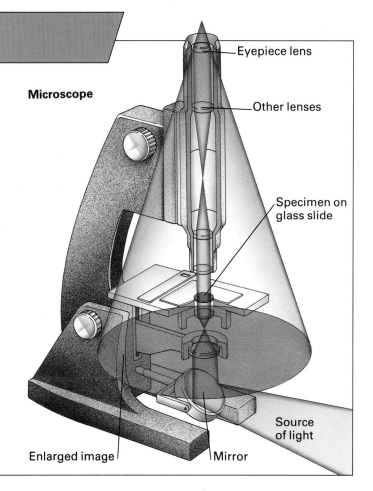

Microscope

- Eyepiece lens
- Other lenses
- Specimen on glass slide
- Source of light
- Enlarged image
- Mirror

Cameras

A simple camera is basically a light-tight box with a hole at the front, called the aperture, covered by a lens. Light entering the lens is focused by it to form an upside-down image on light-sensitive film at the back of the camera. A shutter at the front normally stops light from getting into the camera, but when a picture is being taken the shutter moves aside for a fraction of a second. The lens can usually be moved backward or forward to focus on distant or nearby objects. The amount of light entering the camera – the exposure – is controlled by altering the aperture size or by varying the shutter speed. The photographer looks into a viewfinder to see that the camera is aimed correctly.

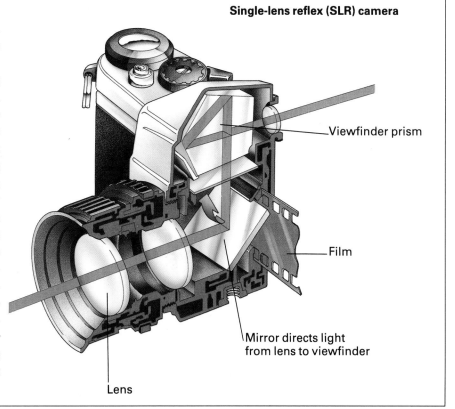

Single-lens reflex (SLR) camera

- Viewfinder prism
- Film
- Mirror directs light from lens to viewfinder
- Lens

LASERS

A laser produces a beam of very pure light in which all the waves are exactly in step and of exactly the same wavelength. The light is produced by atoms, using a principle discovered by Albert Einstein in 1917 but not achieved practically until 1960 by scientists in the United States.

A laser is a device in which atoms are stimulated to amplify a flash of light. The word laser comes from the initials of the phrase Light Amplification by Stimulated Emission of Radiation. The first continuously operating laser was built in 1960 by an American scientist, Theodore Maiman. Laser beams are very narrow and do not spread appreciably as they travel along. They can be used for cutting and welding metal, for performing various kinds of surgery, for making holograms (three-dimensional photographs) and in spectacular laser light shows.

How a laser works

The first lasers used a small cylinder of ruby crystal to produce their light. A powerful flash tube was wrapped around the cylinder, which had a mirror at each end. One of the mirrors had a small unsilvered area at the center. When the flash tube was turned on, the ruby became bathed in light, which its atoms absorbed. After a short time, the atoms could no longer "hold" the absorbed light and they released it again as a bright pulse. Some of this light traveled along the crystal to be reflected between the two mirrors. As this light went through the crystal, it stimulated other atoms to emit more light traveling in step and in the same direction as the original light. In turn, this light stimulated further emission. This powerful light escaped, as a narrow beam, through the center of one mirror.

A laser light show in the United States

WHITE LIGHT

Different wavelengths moving in different directions

LASER LIGHT

Single wavelength moving in same direction in step

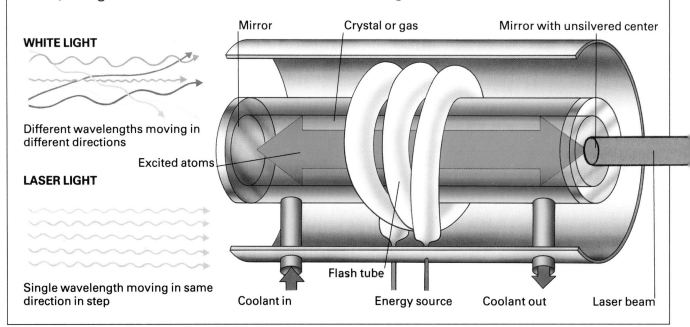

Mirror Crystal or gas Mirror with unsilvered center

Excited atoms

Flash tube

Coolant in Energy source Coolant out Laser beam

Lasers in action

Lasers are used in homes, factories and hospitals. A compact disc or videodisc player contains a low-power laser whose beam reads the signal on the disc, like the stylus reads the music on an ordinary audio disc. Surgeons use lasers to carefully "weld" back a detached retina at the back of the eye or to remove birthmarks or tattoos from the skin. In factories lasers cut and weld metal sheets or slice through a pile of cloth to cut out pieces for making clothes. Surveyors use lasers to measure distances very accurately.

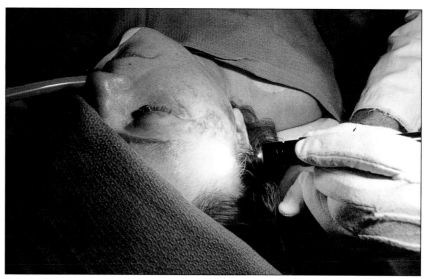

A laser beam being used to remove a birthmark

Holograms

A hologram is a three-dimensional (3-D) photograph produced using laser light. If when viewing a hologram you move your head slightly, you see the scene from a different angle. To make a hologram, light from a laser is shone on the object being photographed. The light is reflected off the object onto a piece of photographic film. At the same time, light from the same laser passes straight to the film. The two beams of light reaching the film produce an interference pattern, which can be seen when the film is developed. If laser light is shone through the film, the pattern becomes a 3-D image.

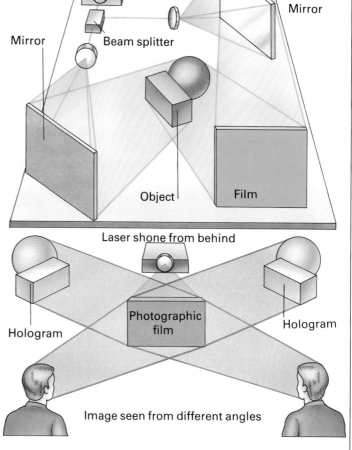

Laser source

Mirror

Mirror

Beam splitter

Object

Film

Laser shone from behind

Hologram

Photographic film

Hologram

Image seen from different angles

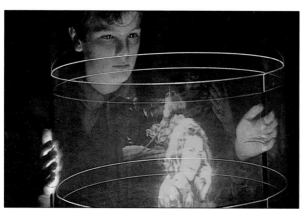

A boy looking at a circular hologram

FIBER OPTICS

Optical fibers consist of flexible strands of glass. Light traveling along a bundle of fibers may be "carrying" an image or may be pulsed in such a way that it is carrying messages. Such images or messages therefore travel at close to the speed of light (300,000 km/186,000 miles per second).

Most telephone messages today are transmitted as electrical signals along copper wires. But only a few messages can be sent along a single wire. Fiber optics is a new system of carrying messages that uses thin strands of glass, called optical fibers, instead of wires. High-speed pulses of laser light, sent through a bundle of fibers can carry hundreds of messages (in the form of television broadcasts, telephone calls or computer data) at the same time. Optical fibers are already being used by telephone companies and are likely to be used more in the future.

Thin glass strands

The thin glass strands in optical fibers are about the thickness of a human hair. They can bend without breaking, so they can carry light around corners. The glass is so pure that a sheet 35 millimeters (1.4 inches) thick would be as transparent as an ordinary window pane ten times as thin.

Most optical fibers are made with a thin outer covering of a different type of glass, which ensures that the light bounces from side to side within the fiber and cannot escape. Thus when light is directed in at one end of the fiber it stays inside and comes out only at the other end. The light is produced by a laser. Sometimes small laser chips are used, which are crystals that give off laser light when electrified.

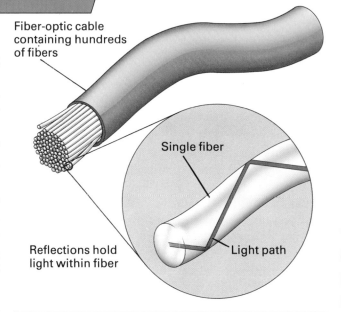

Fiber-optic cable containing hundreds of fibers

Single fiber

Light path

Reflections hold light within fiber

This copper cable can carry 12 telephone signals.

A fiber-optic cable carries thousands of signals.

The endoscope

An endoscope is an instrument that enables a doctor to look inside a patient's body, for instance into the stomach, lungs, bladder, womb or even the knee joint, to detect the presence of disease or other disorder. It contains two long bundles of optical fibers, which are slowly inserted through a natural opening, such as the patient's mouth, or through a small surgical incision. One bundle carries light into a body cavity and illuminates the area to be inspected. The other carries back a picture of the area to the doctor operating the instrument. An endoscope fitted with biopsy forceps can allow a surgeon to remove bits of tissue from the body to be diagnosed. Using this method, a patient does not have to undergo major surgery to carry out the initial examination.

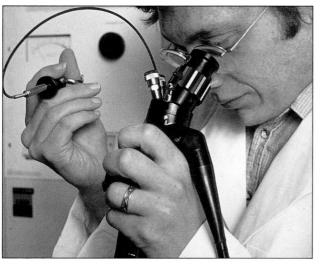

A doctor using a fiber-optic endoscope

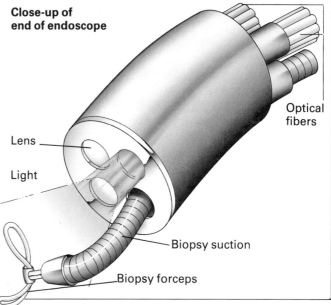

Close-up of end of endoscope

Lens

Light

Optical fibers

Biopsy suction

Biopsy forceps

Talking by light

In the future, telephone conversations will be carried by optical fibers by modulating, or pulsing, the light traveling along them. Optical fibers are not affected by the electrical "noise" that can spoil normal telephone messages. They will also reduce the number of cables needed, because each fiber can carry about 2,000 conversations at the same time (only 30 conversations can be carried on a copper conductor). Optical fibers can also carry television signals, as well as data from one computer to another. Perhaps all homes will eventually have fiber-optic links, carrying TV and radio signals.

Workmen laying fiber-optic cables

UNITS

The area of science, known as physics, is concerned with the various forms of energy. Physics has its own set of units, and they are used for measuring electric currents, the wavelength of light, forces, temperatures, and so on. There is an internationally agreed standard of units called the Système International d'Unités, or SI units for short, based on the meter (for length), kilogram (for mass) and second (for time). Other units can be derived from the basic ones by adding various prefixes that act as multipliers; for instance, the prefix *kilo* stands for a thousand times, so a kilometer is 1,000 meters.

Some SI prefixes

Prefix	Multiplier	Symbol
deci-	x 0.1	d
centi-	x 0.01	c
milli-	x 0.001	m
micro-	x 0.000001	μ
nano-	x 0.000000001	n
pico-	x 0.000000000001	p
tera-	x 1.000,000,000,000	T
giga-	x 1.000,000,000	G
mega-	x 1.000,000	M
kilo-	x 1,000	k
hecto-	x 100	h
deca-	x 10	da

Electricity

Electric current is measured in amperes, amps for short. Volts measure how hard the current is being pushed. Power is expressed in watts, and is the product of the current and the voltage.

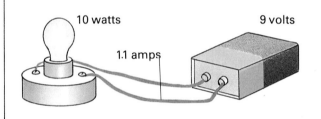

10 watts
9 volts
1.1 amps

Wavelengths

Any wave motion, such as sound, light or a radio signal, has a wavelength equal to the distance between adjacent peaks. Its strength depends on amplitude; the number of waves per second is the frequency.

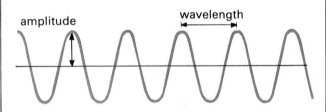

amplitude   wavelength

Mechanics

Mass is usually measured in grams or kilograms; large masses are expressed in metric tons (1 metric ton = 1,000 kilograms). Forces are measured in newtons. Weight is a force, caused by gravity, and a mass of 0.1 kg has a weight of 1 newton. Energy is expressed in joules; 1 joule is the amount of energy used in moving 1 newton a distance of 1 meter.

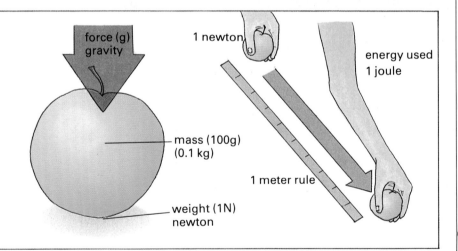

force (g) gravity
1 newton
energy used 1 joule
mass (100g) (0.1 kg)
1 meter rule
weight (1N) newton

Temperature

A measure of an object's hotness, temperature is expressed in degrees Celsius or degrees Fahrenheit. The formulas on the right show how to convert one temperature scale into the other.

To convert °C to °F, use the formula:

°F = (°C X 1.8) + 32

To convert °F to °C, use the formula:

°C = (°F − 32) ÷ 1.8

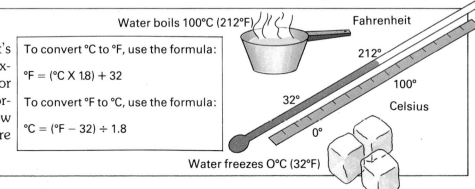

Water boils 100°C (212°F)
Fahrenheit
212°
100°
32°
Celsius
0°
Water freezes 0°C (32°F)

GLOSSARY

absolute zero the lowest possible temperature, equal to 0 K, -273.16 °C or – 459.69 °F.

acceleration the rate of change of velocity.

alternating current an electric current that changes its direction of flow.

atom the smallest amount of a substance that can exist alone and still have the same chemical properties.

center of gravity the point at which an object's mass seems to act.

conduction the movement of heat or electricity through a solid object.

convection the way heat moves through a gas or liquid by a flowing current.

direct current an electric current that flows in one direction only.

electric charge the amount of electricity held on an object; it may be positive or negative.

electromagnetic wave a wave transmitted by electric and magnetic fields that can travel through space; light and radio waves travel as electromagnetic waves.

electron a tiny particle, with a negative charge, that forms part of an atom.

energy the capacity to do work.

force a push or a pull, equal to the product of mass and acceleration.

gamma ray a powerful form of radiation produced by radioactive atoms.

gravity the force that attracts objects to each other because of their mass.

hologram a 3-dimensional image produced by a laser.

infrared light heat rays; the way heat travels through empty space or air.

ion an atom carrying an electric charge (which may be positive or negative).

kinetic energy the energy of movement, determined by an object's mass and velocity.

laser a device that produces a powerful, narrow beam of single-wavelength light.

luminescence light that is not produced by heat.

mass the amount of matter in a substance.

microwave a type of very high-frequency radio wave used in telecommunications and ovens.

molecule a tiny particle of a substance consisting of chemically combined atoms.

momentum the tendency of a moving object to keep moving, equal to the product of its mass and its velocity.

neutron a particle with no electric charge, found in the nucleus of an atom.

nucleus the small, relatively heavy central part of an atom.

phosphor a substance that glows when it is hit by ions or electrons.

potential energy stored energy that is due to the change in shape or position of an object.

primary colors the three colors which when mixed can produce any other color.

proton a particle with a positive electric charge, found in the nucleus of an atom.

radiation energy that can travel as waves through empty space.

refraction the bending of a beam of light as it passes from one transparent substance to another.

spectrum the band of colors produced when white light passes through a prism.

superconductor a material that (at low temperature) has no resistance to an electric current.

surface tension the force that makes the surface of a liquid contract.

ultraviolet ray invisible electromagnetic waves found in sunlight that cause sunburn.

velocity speed, or the rate at which an object is moving in a particular direction.

wavelength the distance between the peak of a wave and the peak of the one following it.

X ray a powerful form of electromagnetic wave that can pass through many materials.

INDEX

All entries in bold are found in the Glossary

Photographic Credits:
l= left, r= right, t = top, b = bottom, m = middle
Cover and pages 8(l), 9(b), 13, 16, 17(t), 25(t), 31(both), 32(both), 33(t) and back cover: Science Photo Library; intro page and pages 8(r), 12(both), 14, 15, and 26 (both): Zefa; pages 6(l) and 7(t & m): NASA; page 6(r): Aerospatiale; page 7(b): LRT

Museum; page 9(t): Frank Spooner Agency; pages 10(l), 19(b) and 28: Robert Harding Library; pages 17 (b), 19 (t) and 27 (b): Vanessa Bailey; page 21: Barnaby's; page 24(t): National Gallery; page 24(b): Bruce Coleman; pages 25(b) and 27(t): Spectrum Colour Library; page 30: Rex Features; page 33(b): Chapel Studios/British Telecom.